ROCK & POP
Classics

Love Hurts

Touching songs of painful love

Love Hurts

The course of true love, as the saying goes, never runs smooth. And the proof is right here on *Love Hurts*. While some relationships are doomed to fail, others cause as much sadness as they do happiness. Infidelity, betrayal, suspicion and hurt dominate those partnerships, as well as this collection of songs devoted to the painful side of human relationships. Heartache and broken lives have had a particular fascination for some of rock music's outstanding songwriters. This volume of *Rock & Pop Classics* gathers together their most perceptive and touching songs—songs which take pain and bitterness and turn them into something strong and everlasting.

THE LISTENER'S GUIDE – WHAT THE SYMBOLS MEAN

THE INSPIRATION
The stories behind the music and artists

THE ARTIST
The lives, the loves... the scandal

THE MUSIC
Why songs sound the way they do

THE BACKGROUND
People, places and events that shape the songs

Contents

ROCK & POP
Classics

Kiss and Say Goodbye
THE MANHATTANS

On a career that has spanned more than 35 years, the suave vocal group the Manhattans enjoyed a dozen R&B hits. The success of their soulful ballads has never been matched by stardom, however. Even in the mid-'70s, when "Kiss and Say Goodbye," with its spoken introduction and classic doo-wop ballad of love gone wrong, topped both the R&B and pop charts, the band kept a relatively low profile.

KINGS OF WOE

Broken hearts and soured relationships were the staple of the Manhattans' ballads. They put the pain of breaking up and loss into words and bittersweet harmonies. The five male voices—female singer Regina Belle joined briefly in the mid-'80s—gave the group's close harmonies a telling depth. Masters of the tearjerker, the band has sold more than 12 million records in its career.

NEW MEMBER, NEW SOUND

The Manhattans' future seemed in jeopardy after lead singer George "Smitty" Smith died of spinal meningitis in 1970. However, the band had met singer Gerald Alston *(left)* at a show in North Carolina, and they asked him to join. With Alston on board, the group's sound became sweeter and silkier, as demonstrated by "Kiss and Say Goodbye." Alston left to launch a solo career in 1988, but this proved unsuccessful. He rejoined the band to celebrate its 30th anniversary.

 ## MANHATTAN-BOUND

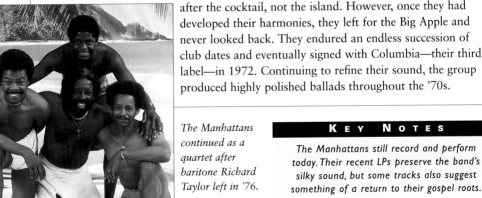

The Manhattans did not actually come from Manhattan *(right),* but from across the Hudson in Jersey City, N.J. In fact, they named themselves after the cocktail, not the island. However, once they had developed their harmonies, they left for the Big Apple and never looked back. They endured an endless succession of club dates and eventually signed with Columbia—their third label—in 1972. Continuing to refine their sound, the group produced highly polished ballads throughout the '70s.

The Manhattans continued as a quartet after baritone Richard Taylor left in '76.

KEY NOTES

The Manhattans still record and perform today. Their recent LPs preserve the band's silky sound, but some tracks also suggest something of a return to their gospel roots.

Bye Bye Love
EVERLY BROTHERS

The first in a long line of hits for the Everly Brothers, "Bye Bye Love" straddled the line between country and rock, climbing to No. 2 on the pop chart and topping the country chart for seven weeks in 1957. "There goes my baby with someone new," sing the duo in this breakup song that includes the vow of the recently jilted: "I'm through with romance, I'm through with love."

BROTHERS IN HARMONY

The Everlys' two-part harmonies were admired and emulated by many subsequent musical greats. Simon and Garfunkel *(left)* covered "Bye Bye Love" on their *Bridge Over Troubled Water* LP, and sang "Wake Up Little Susie" during their 1981 concert in Central Park. Paul McCartney paid tribute to the duo by mentioning them by name on his 1976 Wings hit "Let 'Em In."

BYE BYE DEBT

"Bye Bye Love" was written by the husband-and-wife songwriting team of Felice and Boudleaux Bryant, who also wrote the No. 1 hits "Wake Up Little Susie" and "All I Have to Do Is Dream" for the boys. "Bye Bye Love" was reportedly rejected by 30 different acts before the Everlys agreed to record it. The brothers, hurting for money at the time, both remember getting excited about the $64 session fee they would receive for the recording. The song soon started a buzz in Nashville that stayed with the duo for the next seven years.

KEY NOTES

Phil Everly made an appearance in the Clint Eastwood movie Every Which Way But Loose, *performing with actress Sondra Locke (above).*

BROTHERLY LOVE

Don and Phil Everly *(below)* are the sons of popular country artists Ike and Margaret Everly. Growing up, the boys were regulars on their parents' radio shows and even accompanied their folks on tour. In the mid-'50s, they moved to Nashville and jumped on the burgeoning rockabilly bandwagon. After a string of hits and arena concerts, the Everlys endured a decade of mediocre record sales, stints at smaller venues and mounting tension. The duo's clashes culminated in an on-stage, guitar-smashing fight in 1973. The brothers did not speak to each other for 10 years, and saw each other only at their father's funeral. They reunited in 1983 and have recorded and toured again. They were inducted into the Rock and Roll Hall of Fame in 1986.

I Need You
AMERICA

The harmonizing trio America emerged onto the early '70s folk pop scene with an impressive list of Top 10 hits. The piano-based, plaintive ballad "I Need You," followed the chart-topping "Horse with No Name" as the second single off their self-titled debut album *(above)*. The single surged to No. 9 on the pop chart in 1972. The emotionally-charged song—written by singer/guitarist Gerry Beckley when he was only 16—taps into the fragile feelings of a person who was recently dumped.

AMERICA ABROAD

Dewey Bunnell, Gerry Beckley and Dan Peek were all sons of Air Force officers stationed in England. They met and began playing together in high school. After graduation, the trio auditioned for local music promoter Jeff Dexter, who booked rock concerts at a venue called the Roundhouse. Dexter liked what he heard and got America gigs opening for acts like Elton John and the Who *(right)*. Dexter later coproduced their successful first album.

EARLY '70S BLEND

America's hybrid of folk and rock was typical of music in the early '70s. Bands like the Hollies *(below)*, Crosby, Stills and Nash and the Eagles all used a similar approach—a mixture of acoustic and electric guitars with rich, three-part harmonies. Like those bands, America often dealt with loneliness and heartbreak in their music.

🌐 THE MARTIN TOUCH

George Martin *(below)*, the legendary producer of the Beatles, took a liking to America after hearing their first album and agreed to produce them. Aware of the band's reputation for taking a long time in the studio, he insisted they come to London to record. The trio was so nervous and excited about working with Martin that they rehearsed relentlessly in preparation. They got the songs so tight that they wrapped up recording their first album with Martin in less than three weeks. America was the only band other than the Beatles that Martin ever worked with on a continued basis.

KEY NOTES

The trio allegedly chose their name after listening to an Americana jukebox in a London pub. The name was fitting for the group of Americans who had lived abroad for so long.

Cold as Ice
FOREIGNER

Foreigner brought together American and British musicians to create hard rock with a commercial edge. The combination worked. The group became a huge attraction on the stadium-rock circuit and its singles and LPs stormed the charts. One heavy-metal magazine put it best, hailing Foreigner's ability to write "slushy songs that millions can identify with." Taken from the band's self-titled debut album *(above left)*, "Cold as Ice" chilled at No. 6 in 1977. The song's catchy keyboard phrases, combined with the towering vocals of singer Lou Gramm, turn the story of a frosty reception for a would-be lover into a classic tale of rejection.

🎤 RIOT-TORN REUNION

Lou Gramm was born Lou Grammatico in Rochester, N.Y., in 1950. He sang with a number of hard-rock bands before his bluesy voice convinced guitarist Mick Jones that Gramm was the man to front Foreigner. Jones' songs were a perfect vehicle for Gramm, who sang the band's biggest hits. In 1990, however, he left to form his own group. But when martial law was enforced during the Los Angeles riots of 1992 *(left)*, Gramm and Jones found themselves trapped in a hotel. The pair began writing songs to pass the time, and Gramm rejoined Foreigner later that year.

🌐 COMBINATION FOR SUCCESS

Foreigner were the brainchild of veteran U.K. guitarist Mick Jones, who had a remarkable knack for finding rock success. This owed a lot to talent: Jones was a musicians' musician who later worked with the likes of Eddie Van Halen *(left)*, Billy Joel and Eric Clapton. His triumph was also a sign of experience. He had paid his musical dues for years in Paris, developing the career of French star Johnny Hallyday *(above right)*. Another key to Jones' success is his ability to pen hit songs. He teamed up with Gramm to write every one of Foreigner's Top 40 singles, including "Cold As Ice."

KEY NOTES

In 1995 Foreigner performed for the American Association for Nude Recreation. The open-air concert attracted a vast audience who were all entirely naked.

Think of Laura
CHRISTOPHER CROSS

Anyone who's ever loved and lost can relate to this easy-listening radio smash, a Top 10 single from Christopher Cross' 1983 sophomore album, *Another Page*. Cross' melodic composition and smooth alto voice are a perfect romantic vehicle for this ode to Laura. Her lover, the ballad tells us, lost her when she died too young, but finds comfort in knowing that her memory lives on "in every day we live," so he can remember with a smile instead of tears.

PROUD TO BE POP

Cross once said, "I used to apologize for pop music, but I don't anymore." And pop returned the compliment. Cross' 1980 self-titled debut album went double platinum and helped him earn five Grammys, including Best Album and Best New Artist. He kept up the winning formula of soft rock ballads on his 1983 follow-up *Another Page (left)*, which hit No. 11 on the album chart, thanks in large part to the radio power of "Think of Laura." The album yielded a pair of other Top 40 singles: "All Right" and "No Time for Talk."

⭐ LUKE'S LAMENT

Part of what fueled the success of "Think of Laura" was ABC's use of the song on the soap opera *General Hospital*, as the theme music for the characters Luke and Laura. The star-crossed lovers helped drive viewers to *General Hospital* in record numbers in the mid-'80s, and the ardorous couple's wedding *(left)* remains the highest-rated episode of a daytime drama ever. On the show, Laura is kidnapped shortly after the wedding and taken to an island, while Luke, thinking she's dead, grieves to the refrain of Cross' "Think of Laura." Years later, when the couple was reprised on the show, so was their musical accompaniment.

HELPING HANDS

Cross has collaborated with some of the biggest singer-songwriters around. On his 1980 debut album, he worked with Eagles singer/drummer Don Henley and Doobie Brother Michael McDonald *(right)*, who sang backing vocals on the hit single "Ride Like the Wind." The following year, with the award-winning writing team of Carole Bayer Sager, Burt Bacharach and Peter Allen, Cross penned the Oscar-winning theme song for the movie *Arthur*, starring Dudley Moore. Cross performed the vocals on "Arthur's Theme (Best That You Can Do)," which was included in the cassette release of *Another Page*. "Arthur's Theme" topped the U.S. chart and became Cross' only Top 10 single in Great Britain.

KEY NOTES

Cross' third album, 1985's Every Turn of the World, *was delayed when he broke his hand in an auto racing accident.*

11

At This Moment

BILLY VERA AND THE BEATERS

A heavily R&B-influenced track, "At This Moment" was a minor success in 1981, but reappeared five years later, eventually topping the singles chart for two weeks. With his heartfelt and soulful voice, Billy Vera shows he "ain't too proud to beg" to hold his true love again.

BEATING OUT HITS

A musical jack-of-all-trades, Billy Vera is an accomplished producer, singer, and songwriter whose writing credits include Dolly Parton's

No. 1 country hit "I Really Got the Feeling." But Vera's greatest love is R&B. In 1979 he formed the Beaters *(above)*, a multi-piece band of session players, to play the Troubadour nightclub in Los Angeles. The group soon found a large following on the Southern California club scene. In fact, "At This Moment" is a live recording from a 1981 Beaters' show at the Roxy. With its heavy emphasis on horns, the band's sound owes a big debt to the live R&B of the early '60s.

Television Ties

After topping out at No. 79 in 1981, "At This Moment" got a huge boost when it was featured on two episodes of *Family Ties (below)* in 1986, as a musical backdrop for stars Michael J. Fox and Tracy Pollan. After the show, viewers jammed NBC's phone lines with calls asking about the song. "At This Moment" reappeared in record stores in 1986 and hit No. 1 early the next year. Vera went on to pen the theme song for the show *Empty Nest*, starring Richard Mulligan. As an actor, his roles have included appearances on *Beverly Hills, 90210* and a cameo as himself in the film *Blind Date*.

Skunky Success

Although Billy Vera wrote and sang "At This Moment," his backing band, the Beaters, can take the credit for the soulful instrumentation of the song. The most prominent band

member other than Vera was Jeff "Skunk" Baxter *(above)*, one of the most accomplished session guitarists of the '70s and '80s. Before the Beaters, Baxter had played with Steely Dan, leaving after the 1974 album *Pretzel Logic*. He then joined the Doobie Brothers in time for the No. 1 hits "Black Water" and "What a Fool Believes," before departing in 1979.

 Key Notes

Billy Vera made his big screen acting debut as Pinky Carruthers (right, far right) in the 1984 film Buckaroo Banzai with Jeff Goldblum and Peter Weller.

Who's That Girl
EURYTHMICS

Even the title of "Who's That Girl" seemed to be appropriate for the Eurythmics duo when the single reached No. 21 in 1983. The on-off relationship between singer Annie Lennox and production maestro Dave Stewart was public knowledge, and the song seemed to capture the tension between them: A jealous Lennox longs to satisfy her suspicion, and against a sparse electronic backing, her soulful voice begs to know "just one thing."

✪ SWALLOWING HER PAIN

"Who's That Girl" is one of Annie Lennox's many songs hinting at the painful side of love. She said in 1983: "I actually embrace the idea of being happy…I've had my share of pain, and I probably will in the future. But…it's sculpted me into the person I am."

Lennox (third from left) *dressed as Elvis Presley at the 1984 Grammys to challenge ideals of femininity.*

FIGHTING SEXISM

The Eurythmics loved to play with the public's perceptions of gender. Annie Lennox dressed as a man in part of the "Who's That Girl" video and aroused speculation about her sexuality. MTV blacked out the moment when she took off her long wig—exposing cropped hair—fearing that she was promoting transvestism. But Lennox *(below)* claimed she employed an androgynous look in part to transcend sexism, and to try to

ward off the sometimes demeaning remarks of spectators. "I have received that kind of abuse on stage," she said, "and one has to find a way around it. Of course, you'll never find a way around it. But this helps."

VIDEO APPEAL

The Eurythmics' commercial success depended partly on their talents with music video. The music industry had been energized by the launch of MTV in 1981. Young film producers and directors profited from the vast exposure available for what pop star Adam Ant called "a three-minute Hollywood." Careful to control their visual image, Annie Lennox and Dave Stewart took charge of their early videos. The video for "Who's That Girl" featured Lennox in both male and female guises, while Stewart appeared with female stars such as singer Kiki Dee *(above)*.

KEY NOTES

The video for "Who's That Girl" includes an appearance by Siobhan Fahey—of Bananarama and later Shakespear's Sister—who married Dave Stewart in 1987 (right).

All I Need
JACK WAGNER

(A)ctor-turned-singer Jack Wagner blasted his way onto the music scene with "All I Need," a catchy ballad about an unexpected love affair. "I wasn't looking for true love, but now you're looking at me," sings the rough-voiced Wagner on this unlikely hit, which reached No. 5 on the pop chart in 1985.

BALLARD'S BALLAD

Glen Ballard, who cowrote and produced "All I Need," is a giant in the music industry, though most of his successes have come quietly behind the scenes. Ballard, from Natchez, Miss., cowrote and produced Alanis Morissette's entire *Jagged Little Pill (right)* album, which enjoyed enormous chart success in 1995. He also cowrote and played keyboards on Michael Jackson's No. 1 hit "Man in the Mirror." In addition, Ballard has worked with Aerosmith, Van Halen and Elton John, among countless others.

16

 ## JACK-OF-ALL-SOAPS

Jack Wagner has been one of the most famous faces in the history of soap operas. He's had memorable stints on *Knot's Landing*, *Santa Barbara* and as sleazy Dr. Peter Burns on the steamy nighttime drama *Melrose Place (left)*. But Wagner first made his mark as Frisco Jones, one of the most popular characters on the long-running daytime drama *General Hospital*. He left the show and returned a number of times, each time causing a major stir. "All I Need" was actually written into the story line of *General Hospital*. On the show, Frisco wrote the song as a love poem for Tania Roskov, who later married his brother Tony.

 ## SOAPY SUCCESSES

Wagner was not the only soap opera heartthrob to have success on the pop chart in the '80s. Another *General Hospital* graduate, Rick Springfield *(below)* was by far the most successful. The former Dr. Noah Drake had five Top 10 hits, including the 1981 chart-topper "Jessie's Girl." Michael Damian, known to daytime fans as Danny Romalotti on *The Young and the Restless*, went to No. 1 in 1989 with a remake of the David Essex hit "Rock On."

KEY NOTES

At age 8, Wagner (left) was introduced to the game of golf by his father. Today, he is one of the top golfers on the Celebrity Players Tour, and boasts a low score of 64.

Love Hurts
NAZARETH

Nazareth's "Love Hurts"—the band's only Top 10 single—was, remarkably, the 42nd cover of this familiar song. Earlier versions included a hit by the Everly Brothers and a noteworthy interpretation by country-rocker Gram Parsons. Nazareth's 1975 cover proved to be their breakthrough in the U.S., charting at No. 8. Taken from the album *Hair of the Dog,* the song was also included on their live LP *'SNAZ (above).* The band's raucousness along with Dan McCafferty's tortured vocals gave new energy—but also new levels of pain—to this tale of love's abrasive side.

FIFTIES CLASSICS

"Love Hurts" was written by songster Boudleaux Bryant. Named for a Frenchman who saved his father's life in World War I, Bryant found success writing country songs with his wife, Felice, in the 1950s. Despite their country background, the duo *(above)* penned hits for a wide range of artists, adapting their style to appeal to a broad audience. They also wrote early hits for the Everly Brothers and "Take Me as I Am (or Let Me Go)" for Bob Dylan, among others. The Bryants earned a spot in the Country Music Hall of Fame in 1991. Boudleaux once said of his craft: "Unless you know in your heart that you're great, feel in your bones that you're lucky and think in your soul that God just might let you get away with it, pick something more certain, like chasing the white whale or eradicating the common housefly."

SCOTTISH ROCK

Formed from the Shadettes in Scotland in 1969, Nazareth were rockers from the outset. The four members of the new band quit their day jobs to go on an 18-month tour of their homeland, winning a reputation as the hardest working band in Scotland—and one of the hardest partying. With his expansive vocal range, the band's charismatic

singer, Dan McCafferty *(above)*, could change his raspy voice at will from a growl to a purr. With their abrasive, cheeky bravado and giant guitar riffs, Nazareth made their name in the '70s as a hard-rock live act both in Europe and the U.S.

KEY NOTES

Nazareth's music has inspired a new generation of rockers, including Axl Rose (right) of Guns N' Roses, who covered "Hair of the Dog" on the 1993 album The Spaghetti Incident.

Heartbreaker
DIONNE WARWICK

Dionne Warwick's cool, sophisticated vocals took this catchy tale of betrayed trust—penned by the Bee Gees and with backing vocals from Barry Gibb—to No. 10 in 1983. The song's appeal came from its balance of disco rhythms and the caressing, seductive style of Warwick, one of the top stars of the '60s. "Heartbreaker," from the album of the same name, was the work of a consummate performer who had reached her peak long before—and had stayed there.

PARANORMAL INFLUENCES

New Jersey-born Warwick hit an emotional low in the early '70s. She parted from her songwriters Hal David and Burt Bacharach *(right)*, mourned the death of her husband and had a run of ineffectual albums. At one point, she began spelling her name "Warwicke" after a numerologist said it would bring her luck. Her fascination with the spiritual world continued in the '90s, as she hosted TV's *Psychic Friends Network*.

⭐ WITH A LITTLE HELP FROM HER FRIENDS

Heartbreaker was Warwick's fifth LP in a career rebirth that began when she signed to Arista Records in 1979. The star's flagging career was revived when the label's boss, Clive Davis *(left, on left)*, drafted a team of writers and producers to help, including Barry Manilow *(left, on right)* and Bee Gee Barry Gibb *(below right)*. Warwick thrived when working with other artists, and some of her biggest hits of the '80s were duets—with Johnny Mathis, Luther Vandross and Jeffrey Osborne. On 1985's grammy-winning No. 1 hit "That's What Friends Are For," she sang with Elton John, Gladys Knight and Stevie Wonder.

🌐 FAMILY AFFAIR

Like so many black performers of her generation, Warwick began singing in a gospel choir at her local Baptist church. While studying at the Hart College of Music in Hartford, Conn., she formed the Gospelaires with sister Dee Dee, cousin Cissy Houston *(below center, with daughter Whitney on left)* and friend Doris Troy. The group found work as backup singers, and it was during a Drifters session in 1961 that Warwick first impressed Burt Bacharach, who would write a string of solo hits for her.

KEY NOTES

In 1994 Dionne Warwick, a high-profile supporter of many humanitarian causes, spoke of the damage being done to black youths by gangsta rap, which she called "pornography."

I'd Love You to Want Me
LOBO

Lobo, which means "wolf" in Spanish, was the pseudonym that Florida-based singer-songwriter Roland Kent Lavoie came up with for his largely solo musical projects. Lobo stampeded up the charts in the early 1970s with a string of memorable singles, including "I'd Love You to Want Me." Lobo's heartfelt plea to be loved "the way that it should be" held the No. 2 position for two weeks in 1972.

RETURN OF LOBO

Lobo signed his first solo recording deal with Big Tree Records in 1971. The same year, his self-penned single "Me and You and a Dog Named Boo"—a classic road song that tells the tale of a man, his car and his dog—made the Top 5 on both sides of the Atlantic. His 1972 album, *Of a Simple Man*, included a pair of Top 10 hits, "I'd Love You to Want Me" and the bittersweet breakup song "Don't Expect Me to Be Your Friend." In 1979, Lobo made a slight comeback with the No. 23 single "Where Were You When I Was Falling in Love."

SIMPLE SOUNDS

This song is a classic example of less being more in pop music. It starts with an elementary guitar strum and Lobo's pleasant, though imperfect voice, then builds steadily with piano, heavy percussion and female backing singers chiming in on the chorus. Lobo's understated singing style helps portray him as an underdog that the audience can rally behind as he sings "Baby, I'd love you to want me...."

KEY NOTES

Lobo has heard his songs performed by everyone from Perry Como to the Brady Bunch (above), who covered "I'd Love You to Want Me" on their Phonographic album.

LEGENDARY START

Lavoie, who was born in July 1943, was a member of a number of bands in and around his hometown of Winter Haven, Fla. He started out in a band called the Rumors and then jumped over to the Legends, who enjoyed only modest success before breaking up. But years later, it's hard to imagine why the band didn't make it big. Along with Lavoie, the Legends included other future music notables Gram Parsons and Jim Stafford. Parsons *(below right)* was an influential rocker as a member of the Byrds and the Flying Burrito Brothers, before dying of a drug overdose in 1973.

Jim Stafford was best known for his zany, country-flavored singles like "Spiders and Snakes" and "Wildwood Weed," both of which hit the Top 10 in 1974. Lavoie coproduced both songs, along with many of Stafford's other hits.

Never Tear Us Apart

INXS

On 1988 Australian import INXS peaked at No. 7 with the slightly anguished ballad "Never Tear Us Apart," the last in a string of four Top 10 hits from the multi-platinum album *Kick*. A departure from the band's previous hits, the song features an uncharacteristic string arrangement, Kirk Pengilly's blaring saxophone and the distinctive wail of singer Michael Hutchence.

 ### LIKE A ROLLIN' STONE

Although INXS were associated with the waning new wave movement, the band's influences were rooted in the bluesy sound of the Rolling Stones. Despite having a synthesizer on board, the band was still able to mount a discernible rock edge.

Hutchence possessed a captivating stage presence and swaggering strut that could only be compared to that of Mick Jagger *(above)*. In fact, it was often suggested that Hutchence would one day unseat his mentor as rock's most outrageous frontman.

NEED YOU TONIGHT

Michael Hutchence certainly lived the rock 'n' roll cliché, approaching life with a true "in excess" attitude. The tabloid press were particularly interested in Hutchence's eventful love life. In the early '90s, the charismatic singer enjoyed a very public fling with fellow Australian Kylie Minogue. The affair helped the former soap opera starlet-cum-pop singer reinvent herself as a full-on rock chick. After Kylie, Hutchence got together with Danish supermodel Helena Christensen in 1993. This glamorous relationship ended when Hutchence set his sights on Paula Yates, then wife of former Boomtown Rat and Band Aid founder Bob Geldof. In 1996 Yates and Hutchence (*right*) had a daughter, Heavenly Hiraani Tigerlily, but the couple's stormy romance ended in 1997 with Hutchence's mysterious death in a Sydney hotel room.

FARRISS AFFAIR

As a Sydney schoolboy, Michael Hutchence, born in 1962, had a habit of getting into fights. One such fracas was broken up by Andrew Farriss (*right*). Finding they shared a love of rock music, the pair put together a band. Farriss recruited his brothers Jon and Tim, their friend Kirk Pengilly and bass player Garry Beers. The Farriss Brothers, as the band was then known, spent 18 months in Perth rehearsing themselves into a tightly knit rock outfit. They officially became INXS in 1979, and spent the next four years building a significant fan base on the Australian pub circuit. The band eventually found success overseas, hitting the U.S. chart for the first time in 1983 with "The One Thing."

KEY NOTES

A roadie suggested the name In Excess which the band adapted to INXS. There was some concern at the outset that the public might incorrectly pronounce the tag "inks."

After the Love Has Gone
EARTH, WIND & FIRE

A supergroup in both size and impact, the nine-piece band Earth, Wind & Fire *(below)* had a series of hits in the late '70s. The polished, mid-tempo "After the Love Has Gone"—their fourth million-selling single in a row—dripped with emotion, thanks to Philip Bailey's sweet lead vocals and the band's typically exotic sounds. From the acclaimed 1979 *I Am* album, "After the Love Has Gone" rose all the way to No. 2 on both the pop and R&B charts, and earned the band a pair of Grammy awards.

AFRICAN HYBRID

The name Earth, Wind & Fire reflects founder Maurice White's passionate interest in astrology and other mystical beliefs. Early trips to North Africa also ignited his deep fascination with ancient Egypt and all aspects of Egyptology, often represented by the inclusion of pyramids and other imagery on the band's album sleeves. White was inspired to learn the kalimba *(above)*, a small African finger piano that became the band's trademark sound. EW&F took the funk soul of George Clinton and James Brown, added their own special touches, and then refined and "Africanized" this mixture into an internationally popular sound.

STUNNING EXHIBITIONISTS

Founded in 1970 by percussionist and vocalist Maurice White, Earth, Wind & Fire became one of the largest, most theatrical pop bands ever. Although they were technically skilled musicians and their songs contained positive spiritual messages, entertainment was always the key to their success. Outrageous costumes—bright jumpsuits with African motifs—were matched by an extravagant live show *(right)*. Band members levitated, pianos floated in midair and pioneering lasers far outshone any contemporary light show.

 ## MIXING WITH THE ELITE

Maurice White *(below)* was born in Memphis in 1941. As a teenager, he played drums with his former schoolmate, the legendary Booker T. Jones, and later attended the Chicago Conservatory of Music. In the mid-'60s, he became a hot studio drummer for Chess Records in Chicago, where he played on albums for everyone from the Impressions *(right)* to Muddy Waters. But it

was in the late '60s that White realized his true vision when he started Earth, Wind & Fire, a band that found its musical niche somewhere between jazz, funk and R&B.

KEY NOTES

Maurice White once summed up Earth, Wind & Fire's fusion of spirituality and entertainment: "We came out here to try to render a service to mankind, not to be stars. We are actually being used as tools by the Creator."

Maggie May
ROD STEWART

Although it started out as a B-side, "Maggie May" went on to become a classic. A No. 1 on both sides of the Atlantic in 1971, the hit was powered by a folksy feel—aided by a mandolin—and Rod Stewart's own instantly recognizable voice. The song tells the story of a young man's sexual education at the hands of an older woman and how it now must end. Acoustic and electric, folksy and bluesy, innocent and seedy, the song acquired an anthem status which it has never lost.

LAST-MINUTE HIT

Stewart recorded "Maggie May" in just two takes. He recalled: "I was nearly persuaded to take that off the album. A mate…said he didn't think it had anything melodic to offer. I sort of agreed with him, but it was too late because we didn't have any more tracks…When it came out on a single, it was a B-side…And it was a disc jockey in Cleveland, I believe, that turned it over. Otherwise, I wouldn't be here today. I'd still be digging graves in the cemetery."

🎤 FROM SOCCER TO SINGING

Born in London in 1945, Rod first showed promise as a soccer player. However, hopes that he might turn pro soon fizzled. Impressed by his drunken singing in a train station, musician Long John Baldry asked Stewart to join his band in 1963. During his career, Stewart remained as famous for his love for soccer as for his celebrity girlfriends, including Swedish actress Britt Ekland *(right)* and his future wife, model Rachel Hunter.

🜨 ABOUT FACES

When Stewart recorded "Maggie May" he was still a member of the Faces, an R&B band which also included future Rolling Stones guitarist Ron Wood. Stewart proved an effective solo artist and an outstanding songwriter. "Maggie May"—which prominently featured the mandolin of Ray Jackson *(below)*—was the beginning of a series of well-observed love songs. With Stewart's solo success, however, tension grew within the Faces. Bassist Ronnie Lane, in particular, resented the attention the singer received, and quit the group in 1973. Stewart himself left two years later.

Before becoming a singer, Stewart was a grave digger. As a form of initiation, his fellow workers allegedly buried him alive in a locked coffin—temporarily, of course.

Credits & Acknowledgements

PICTURE CREDITS

Cover/IFC/Title and Contents Pages/IBC: Image Bank (F. Jorez) **Page 2:** Archive Photos (F. Driggs) **Page 3:** (CR) Images Colour Library, (BL) London Features International Ltd. (TL) Archive Photos (F. Driggs) **Page 4:** (TR) Archive Photos, (BL) Gamma Liason (B. Laforet) **Page 5:** (BL) Kobal Collection, (CR) Gamma Liason (Krasner/Trebitz) **Page 6:** (B) Retna (A. Kent) **Page 7:** (BR) Pictorial Press, (TC) Shooting Star, (BR) London Features International Ltd. **Page 8:** C. Zlotnik **Page 9:** (CR & BL) Redferns (J-P Leloir and L. Resnick), (TL) Rex Features/Sipa Press (C. Leroy) **Page 10:** (TR) London Features International Ltd. (R. Wolfsen) **Page 11:** (CR) Everett Collection, (BL) Pictorial Press (G. Sosio), (TR) London Features International Ltd. (R. Wolfsen) **Page 12:** (BL & TR) Alfa Records **Page 13:** (BL) Shooting Star, (TR) Michael Ochs (R. McCaffrey), (BR) Twentieth Century Fox **Page 14:** (TL & BR) London Features International Ltd. **Page 15:** (BL) Redferns (P. Cronin), (BR & TR) London Features International Ltd. **Page 16:** (BL) Star File Photo (T. Kaplan) **Page 17:** (TL) Shooting Star, (BL) London Features International Ltd. (G. De Guire), (BR) Star File Photo (L. Paladino)

Page 18: (B) Relay Photos **Page 19:** (TL) Redferns (Glenn A. Baker Archives), (CR) Redferns, (CR Bkgd.) STB (Still Moving Picture Co.), (BR) Corbis (N. Preston) **Page 20:** (R) Rex Features (R. Young), (BL) Redferns (CA) **Page 21:** (TL) Retna (D. Lewis), (CR) Corbis (D. Hogan), (BL) Retna (L. Bisacca) **Page 22:** (R) Shooting Star (Y. Kahana) **Page 23:** (TL) Michael Ochs, (BL) Shooting Star, (CR) Redferns (G. Baker) **Page 24:** (BL) Star File Photo, (TR) Everett Collection **Page 25:** (BL) Globe Photos (D. Norgan), (TR) London Features International Ltd., **Page 26:** (B) Redferns, (TR) Jak Kilby **Page 27:** (TR) Redferns, (CR) Michael Ochs, (BL) London Features International Ltd. **Page 28:** (L) London Features International Ltd. **Page 29:** (TL) London Features International Ltd., (TR & BR) Pictorial Press

Artwork: **John See**

The Publisher has made every effort to obtain the copyright holders' permission for the use of the pictures which have been supplied by the sources listed above, and undertakes to rectify any accidental omissions.